D1611675

Our Baby

(place baby's
photo here)

a Baby Journal

This journal is part of **the Gift of an Angel**
product collection, inspired by the well loved gift book,
the Gift of an Angel, for parents welcoming a new child,
written and illustrated by Marianne Richmond.

©2001 by Marianne Richmond Studios, Inc.
All rights reserved. No part of this book
may be reproduced in any form without
written permission from the publisher.

Marianne Richmond Studios, Inc.
420 N. 5th Street, Suite 840
Minneapolis, MN 55401
www.mariannerichmond.com

ISBN 0-9652-4484-9

Text and illustrations by Marianne Richmond

Book design by Sara Dare Biscan

Printed in China

Second Printing

This is the story

of

_____

Created with love by

_____

Anticipation

Hearing the News

Date _____

Thoughts _____

_____

_____

_____

_____

_____

_____

_____

_____

_____

_____

_____

_____

Sneak Peek

(place
sonogram
photo here)

Date _____

Thoughts _____

_____

_____

Decorating your Room

Names we Liked

For a Boy _____

_____

For a Girl _____

_____

And why we picked yours...

_____

_____

_____

_____

_____

Baby's Shower

(Date, Host, Place, Guests, Gifts)

(special
photos)

A Letter to My Child

Dear Precious Child,

_____

_____

_____

_____

_____

_____

_____

_____

_____

_____

_____

_____

With Love,

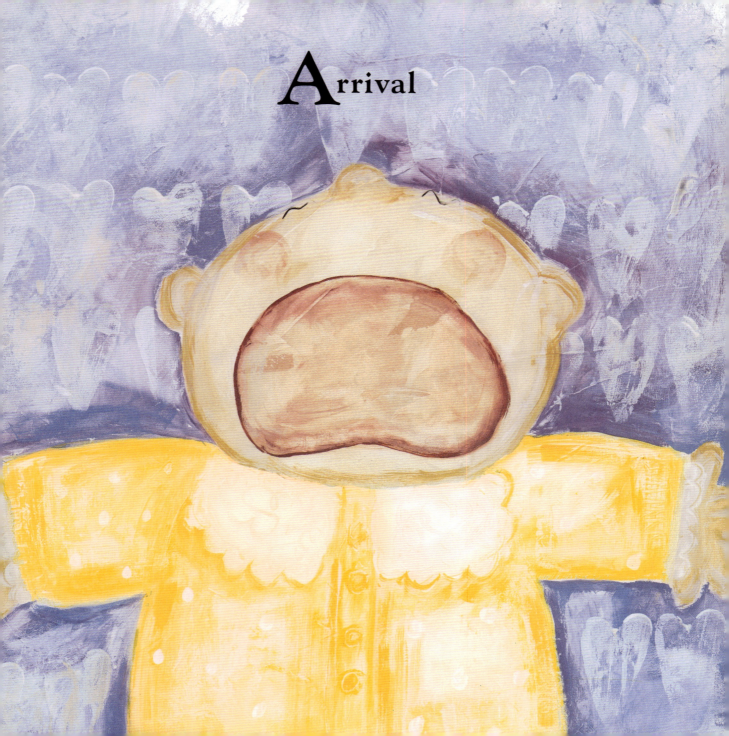

Welcome Little One

Baby's Full Name

_____

Date _____ **Time** _____

Place _____

Weight _____ **Length** _____

Pure Adorable

Eye Color _____

Hair Color _____

Who baby looks like _____

_____

_____

Who was there _____

_____

_____

_____

Birth Certificate

(paste birth
certificate
here)

Tiny Feet, Tiny Hands

Announcement

(paste baby
announcement
here)

First Photos

Homecoming

Baby Comes Home

Where we lived _____

_____

_____

First night home story _____

_____

_____

_____

_____

_____

_____

_____

_____

First Weeks

(Sleeping, Eating, Crying, Visiting)

Family Tree

Great Grandfather	Great Grandmother	Great Grandfather	Great Grandmother
Birthplace, Date	Birthplace, Date	Birthplace, Date	Birthplace, Date

Grandfather	Grandmother
Birthplace, Date	Birthplace, Date

Father

Birthplace, Date

Aunt/Uncle	Aunt/Uncle	Aunt/Uncle	Aunt/Uncle
Birthplace, Date	Birthplace, Date	Birthplace, Date	Birthplace, Date

Family Tree

Great Grandfather	Great Grandmother		Great Grandfather	Great Grandmother
Birthplace, Date	Birthplace, Date		Birthplace, Date	Birthplace, Date

Grandfather	Grandmother
Birthplace, Date	Birthplace, Date

Mother

Birthplace, Date

Aunt/Uncle	Aunt/Uncle		Aunt/Uncle	Aunt/Uncle
Birthplace, Date	Birthplace, Date		Birthplace, Date	Birthplace, Date

Spiritual Celebration

(Event, Officials, Sponsors and Guests)

First Visitors

Discoveries

Firsts

Recognized Parents _____

Smiles _____

Found your Toes _____

Sat up Alone _____

Ate solid Food _____

Firsts

Crawled _____

Pulled up on Furniture _____

First Tooth _____

First Steps _____

First Words _____

Baby's First Haircut

(special
photos)

Lock of Baby's Hair

Thoughts _____

_____

_____

_____

_____

Favorite Things

(Clothes, Toys, Books, Activities)

_____

_____

_____

_____

_____

_____

_____

_____

_____

_____

_____

First Friends

(special
photos)

Growing

1st Month

(special
photos)

Memorable Events and Activities

2nd Month

(special
photos)

Memorable Events and Activities

_____

_____

_____

_____

_____

_____

_____

_____

_____

_____

_____

_____

_____

_____

3rd Month

(special
photos)

Memorable Events and Activities

_____

_____

_____

_____

_____

_____

_____

_____

_____

_____

_____

_____

_____

4th Month

(special
photos)

Memorable Events and Activities

5th Month

(special
photos)

Memorable Events and Activities

_____

_____

_____

_____

_____

_____

_____

_____

_____

_____

_____

_____

_____

6th Month

(special
photos)

Memorable Events and Activities

_____

_____

_____

_____

_____

_____

_____

_____

_____

_____

_____

_____

_____

_____

7th Month

(special
photos)

Memorable Events and Activities

_____

_____

_____

_____

_____

_____

_____

_____

_____

_____

_____

_____

_____

8th Month

(special
photos)

Memorable Events and Activities

9th Month

(special
photos)

Memorable Events and Activities

_____

_____

_____

_____

_____

_____

_____

_____

_____

_____

_____

_____

_____

_____

10th Month

(special
photos)

Memorable Events and Activities

_____

_____

_____

_____

_____

_____

_____

_____

_____

_____

_____

_____

_____

11th Month

(special
photos)

Memorable Events and Activities

_____

_____

_____

_____

_____

_____

_____

_____

_____

_____

_____

_____

12th Month

(special
photos)

Memorable Events and Activities

_____

_____

_____

_____

_____

_____

_____

_____

_____

_____

_____

_____

_____

_____

Milestones

First Major Holiday

(How it was celebrated, guests)

(special
photos)

First Birthday

(How it was celebrated, guests)

(special
photos)

Progress Chart

Month	Weight	Length	Comments
1			
2			
3			
4			
5			
6			

Month	Weight	Length	Comments
7			
8			
9			
10			
11			
12			

Health Records

Shots _____ Date _____
_____

Shots _____ Date _____
_____

Shots _____ Date _____
_____

Shots _____ Date _____
_____

Illnesses / Doctor Visits

Reason _____ Date _____

_____

Reason _____ Date _____

_____

Reason _____ Date _____

_____

Reason _____ Date _____

_____

Reason _____ Date _____

_____